A STUDIO PRESS BOOK

First published in the UK in 2020 by Studio Press,
an imprint of Bonnier Books UK,
The Plaza, 535 King's Road, London SW10 0SZ

www.studiopressbooks.co.uk
www.bonnierbooks.co.uk

1 3 5 7 9 10 8 6 4 2

ISBN 978-1-78741-527-0

Written by Marilyn Easton
Illustrated by Disney Storybook Art Team
Edited by Sophie Blackman
Designed by Rob Ward

A CIP catalogue for this book is available from the British Library
Printed and bound in Poland

Olaf Is Missing!

Olaf and his best friends are travelling all over Arendelle, from Wandering Oaken's Trading Post and Sauna to the Enchanted Forest. Can you spot them in each location?

OLAF

Sweet and innocent, Olaf is a snowman who loves warm hugs and learning about the world around him. He makes new friends wherever he travels and enjoys going on adventures with Elsa, Anna, Kristoff and Sven.

ELSA

As a child, Elsa had to hide her magical snow powers from everyone. But now, with the support of her sister, Anna, she has overcome her fears and fully embraces these powers.

ANNA

Adventurous and kind, Anna is a caring friend. She is determined to protect her family and kingdom, no matter how dangerous a situation may be.

KRISTOFF

At times he may be a little rough around the edges, but Kristoff has a soft spot in his heart for his friends and his one true love, Anna. For a long time Kristoff's only pal was his reindeer, Sven, and though some things have changed over the years, they are still inseparable.

SVEN

Kristoff's best friend and loyal companion, Sven, is a reliable reindeer who will always help his friends when they're in trouble. Though Sven doesn't speak, Kristoff goes to him for advice when he has an important decision to make.

LOCATIONS

Look out for Olaf and his friends as they travel through the kingdom of Arendelle and beyond! In each location, you'll find Olaf, Elsa, Anna, Kristoff and Sven as they attend a festive gathering, embark on a voyage, shop at Wandering Oaken's Trading Post and Sauna or play in the snow. For even more characters and objects to look for in each scene, turn to page 34.

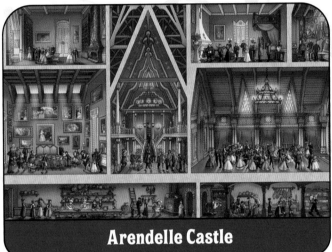

Arendelle Castle

The Great Hall

Arendelle Castle Courtyard

Ice Rink

Marketplace

Wandering Oaken's Trading Post and Sauna

Arendelle Village

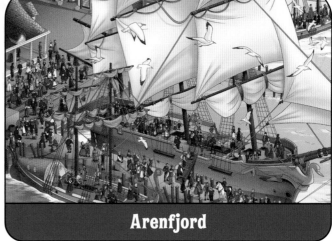

Arenfjord

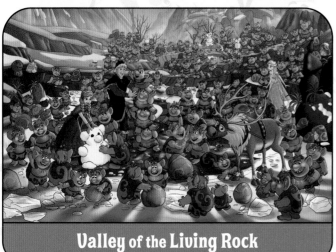

Valley of the Living Rock

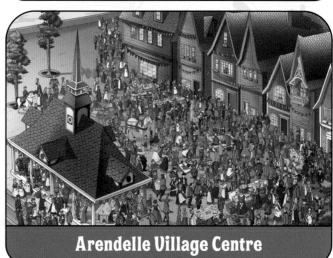

Arendelle Village Centre

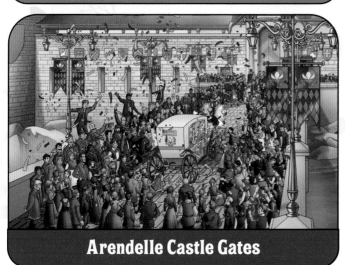

Arendelle Castle Gates

The Mountains

The Enchanted Forest

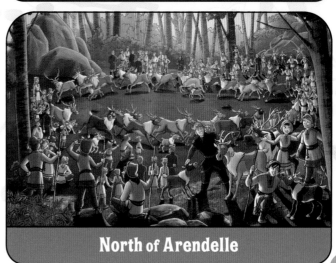

North of Arendelle

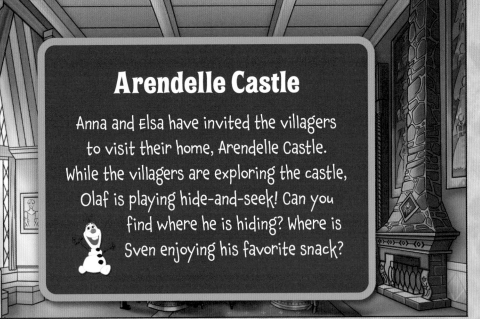

Arendelle Castle

Anna and Elsa have invited the villagers to visit their home, Arendelle Castle. While the villagers are exploring the castle, Olaf is playing hide-and-seek! Can you find where he is hiding? Where is Sven enjoying his favorite snack?

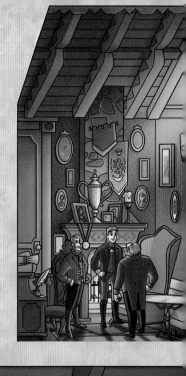

The Great Hall

Olaf and his friends are hosting a festive occasion in the Great Hall. There are couples dancing, musicians performing and a table full of delicious desserts. What is Anna doing? Can you find Olaf among the elegant guests?

Arendelle Castle Courtyard

The villagers have gathered in the courtyard to hear a special announcement from Elsa. Can you spot Olaf and his friends in the crowd? Who is holding the door open, welcoming guests inside?

Ice Rink

At the outdoor ice rink, some people are skating and doing tricks while others are playing in the snow. Can you spot playful Olaf among the villagers? Is Elsa skating or chatting with a friend?

Marketplace

It's a bustling day at the marketplace. The streets are filled with happy customers buying goods from friendly vendors. Can you find Olaf and his friends shopping with the villagers? Which of Olaf's friends are holding baskets?

Wandering Oaken's Trading Post and Sauna

Oaken is having his biggest blowout sale yet! Villagers from all over Arendelle have arrived to find a good bargain. As Oaken welcomes guests to his shop, can you spot Olaf in the crowd?

Arendelle Village

The villagers of Arendelle are enjoying a crisp winter evening with their neighbours and friends. Where is Olaf on this chilly night? Can you spot Anna in the crowd? Which of Olaf's friends are watching the festivities from a window?

Arenfjord

Bon voyage! Olaf is about to depart for an adventure on the high seas. As the ships prepare for the long journey ahead, can you find Olaf, Sven and Kristoff? Who is waving goodbye to Olaf from the shore?

Valley of the Living Rock

Olaf, Kristoff, Sven, Elsa and Anna have just arrived at the Valley of the Living Rock. They are excited to spend time with Kristoff and Sven's troll family. Who is Olaf playing with? Can you find wise Grand Pabbie?

Arendelle Village Centre

It's the Harvest Festival, and the Village Centre is filled with villagers enjoying a feast, dancing and gathering with friends. Is Olaf dancing with Anna or is he listening to a story? Can you spot Olaf's friends enjoying the festival?

Arendelle Castle Gates

Olaf, Anna and Elsa are arriving at Arendelle Castle after a long journey. A large crowd is gathered outside the castle gates to greet them. Where is Olaf? Can you find Sven and Kristoff among the Arendellians?

The Mountains

It's a snowy day in the mountains and the local villagers are enjoying sledging, building snowmen and having snowball fights! How is Olaf spending his time in the wintry weather? Can you spot Elsa?

The Enchanted Forest

In the Enchanted Forest, the Arendellian soldiers and Northuldra are greeting Elsa, Anna, Olaf, Kristoff and Sven. Is Olaf giving Sven a carrot or talking with a new friend? Where is Elsa?

North of Arendelle

Just outside of the Enchanted Forest, reindeer are playfully prancing amid the Northuldra and Arendellian soldiers. Which spirit of nature is swirling around Olaf? Can you find Elsa, Anna, Kristoff and Sven?

Look out for these extra characters and objects:

Arendelle Castle (page 6-7)
- Carrot
- Water pitcher
- Loaf of bread
- Vase with flowers
- King Agnarr

The Great Hall (page 8-9)
- Cupcakes
- Lute
- Glasses
- Purple gloves
- Fan

Arendelle Castle Courtyard
(page 10-11)
- Woman holding a blue bag
- Green bow
- Boys talking
- Blue hat
- Yellow waistcoat

Ice Rink (page 12-13)
- Snowman wearing a hat
- Scarf
- Snowshoes
- Sledge
- Snowball

Marketplace (page 14-15)
- Bread
- Pumpkin
- Eggs
- Baby
- Scale

Wandering Oaken's Trading Post and Sauna (page 16-17)
- Troll statue
- Lantern
- Rake
- Girl holding a ball
- Bottle

Arendelle Village (page 18-19)
- Chimney
- White cat
- Shovel
- Basket of sticks
- Yellow scarf

Answers

Olaf, Anna, Elsa, Kristoff and Sven are circled in red, and the other characters and objects to search for are circled in green.

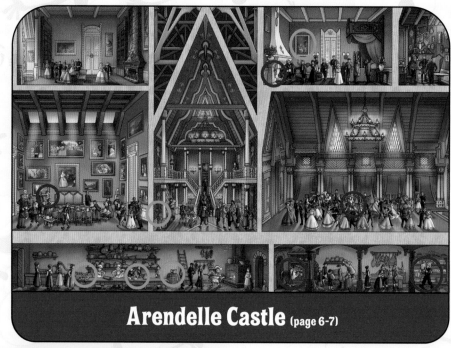

Arendelle Castle (page 6-7)

The Great Hall (page 8-9)

Arendelle Castle Courtyard (page 10-11)

Ice Rink (page 12-13)

Marketplace (page 14-15)

Wandering Oaken's Trading Post and Sauna
(page 16-17)

Arendelle Village (page 18-19)

Arenfjord (page 20-21)

Valley of the Living Rock (page 22-23)

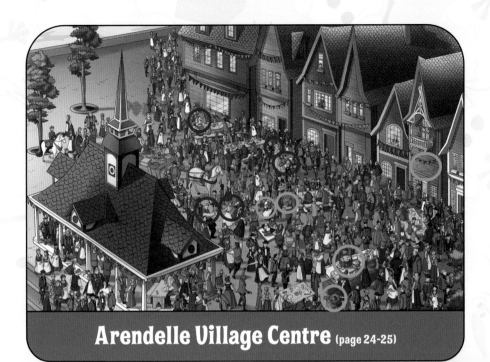

Arendelle Village Centre (page 24-25)

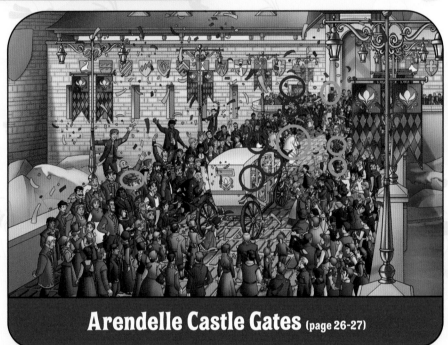

Arendelle Castle Gates (page 26-27)

The Mountains (page 28-29)

The Enchanted Forest (page 30-31)

North of Arendelle (page 32-33)